NATURE'S HABITATS

BY JEROME A. JACKSON

PHOTOGRAPHY
Bates Littlehales

Starwood Publishing, Inc.
Washington, D.C.

Designed by Megan Rickards Youngquist

Edited by Owen Andrews and Carolyn M. Clark

Developed by C. Douglas Elliott

Photographs copyright © 1991 by Bates Littlehales. All rights reserved.

Copyright © 1991 by Starwood Publishing, Inc.

All rights reserved.

No part of the contents of this book may be reproduced

without the written permission of the publisher.

ISBN 0-912347-78-3

Printed in Japan by Dai Nippon Printing Ltd.

5 4 3 2 1   98 97 96 95 94 93 92 91

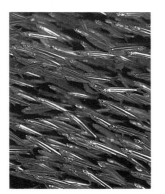

NATURE'S
HABITATS

(Facing) Dudleya clings to life on the slopes of California's sometimes harsh Pacific coast. Lodging in cracks in the rock, the plant is so well suited to its habitat that one of its nicknames is "live forever." Another, "hen and chickens," describes the profusion of younger plants around each matriarch.

ll's right with the world," our politicians tell us. "We are taking steps to protect our environment." But if we ask them to explain what's being protected, the environment they allude to seems remote and nebulous. Maybe the word "environment" is part of the problem. Its meaning is so general, and it has become such a buzz word, that anyone can toss it around without fear of having promised anything.

An environment of some sort will always surround us. It may be one that neither we nor any other species care to inhabit. The word has a neutral sound; it can describe any set of conditions, however positive or negative.

Before "environment" became a popular word, we talked about "ecology." Coined from two Greek words, *oikos*, meaning "house," and *logos*, meaning "study," the term implies that the natural world is a kind of household where each inhabitant's actions affect everyone else. As ecology became a familiar topic, we learned that in Earth's

household, one family member was making a very big difference. A small example: DDT and PCBs, poisonous chemicals manufactured and used in the industrial nations of the northern hemisphere, were being found in the tissues of penguins in the Antarctic and polar bears in the Arctic.

Thinking ecologically, thinking about a worldwide interdependent community, certainly raised the level of discussion. According to a recent *National Geographic* article, our understanding of the relations between living things used to be so limited that in the 1940s, lumber companies convincingly described mature virgin forests as decadent places where living species didn't prosper. Clear-cutting, they said, stimulated natural growth and competition.

The lumber companies' economic goals have often blinded them to the ecological value of the forests they consume. Where they have seen tree trunks rotting on the ground, useless as timber, naturalists perceive a vigorous community of animals, insects, plants, and fungi. All are making use of the dead wood, and all are contributing to the life of the forest around them. Where lumbermen have seen groves of mature but silent trees, rich in board feet for houses and pulp for newspapers, naturalists discern the framework of a bustling household, its leafy branches a roof against extremes of sun and weather.

A good word to describe a place like that, a stable home for wild things, is "habitat." The environment is everywhere; a habitat is in a specific place. You can go to a habitat, study it, make pictures of it, describe it to others. Maybe, if the right people are listening, you can even help protect it against harmful changes.

This book is about natural habitats, the places where wild plants and animals *can* live: forests, grasslands, deserts, ponds and streams, marshes, estuaries, and edges, the interfaces between different kinds of habitats.

Habitats are the places where wild animals and plants feel at home. Just as a home is not simply a manmade structure, a habitat is not simply a place on a map. Just as a house is not a home unless a family lives there, a place is not a habitat except in reference to the plants and animals that occupy it. When naturalists talk about habitat, they mean both a distinct place and the plants and animals which thrive there.

Marsh habitat, for example, is more than an area submerged in shallow water. It is a community of mutually dependent plants and animals. Each has its own needs in that marsh. Some of these needs overlap; others are totally independent; still others may conflict. Bullfrogs and egrets both live in marsh habitats; they depend on the presence of water. Both feed on the marsh's plentiful insect population. When they nest, they choose different parts of the marsh. The egret builds its nest in a nearby tree, while the bullfrog deposits its eggs underwater. To this portrait of peaceful coexistence, we must add an element of gory competition. Given the chance, the egret happily seizes and eats the bullfrog.

Habitats are thus creature-specific places that include both physical and living components. And the whole of one creature's habitat may be just a fragment of another's. The bullfrog is limited to the waters of one marsh; the egret's habitat includes adjacent fields and marshes.

"Niche" is the word that is often used to explain how each species occupies its habitat. Its meaning encompasses the full range of a species' needs and activities. A niche has spatial qualities. How large an area does an individual plant or animal need? It has temporal qualities. When is the plant or animal active? It has interactive qualities. What does the plant or animal eat and what eats it? It has chemical and physical qualities. What are the plant or animal's tolerances of temperature, acidity, light, wind, water, and aridity? It has social qualities. How tolerant is the species to crowding or isolation? The list could go on. Any factor which has an influence on the survival of a species has an influence in shaping its niche. The niche, in turn, defines the limits of a species' habitat.

In a sense, this book is as much about niches as it is about habitats. Because habitats are places, we can easily visualize, categorize, and catalogue them if we wish. Niches are so multidimensional, so abstract, so variable with habitat conditions, season, and the genetic makeup of a population that they can be difficult to deal with. Today, when protecting rare and valuable niches and habitats usually means a loud political struggle, it is easier to sell someone the idea of protecting a place—a habitat—than a niche, which can't be shown on a map. If we can have the habitat, then we can have the plants and animals within it, each with its own niche. You can't protect a niche without the habitat, but you can't understand the habitat without appreciating the niches of the plants and animals that call that habitat home.

Just as species in their niches interact to create a habitat, habitats fit into larger interacting patterns which we call "ecosystems." In an ecosystem, different habitats share a common framework of climate and topography. For example, the grassland

(Facing) One of North America's smallest songbirds, the ruby-crowned kinglet, endures harsh cold by fluffing its feathers and trapping an insulating layer of air next to its body. A regular member of midwinter mixed foraging flocks, it digs hibernating insects, spiders, and their eggs from the bark of woodland trees and shrubs.

ecosystem of the American Great Plains includes habitats that differ in the species of dominant grass, the type of soil, the amount of rainfall, the frequency of fire, and many other features.

Major changes in one ecosystem may affect its neighbors. When hardwood forests are stripped from the coast of a tropical island, a forest community dies. What's more, the next monsoon will sluice the now-exposed topsoil onto coral reefs in the surrounding sea, suffocating delicate marine organisms and shattering the balance of that ecosystem. From niche to niche, from habitat to habitat, from ecosystem to ecosystem, the webs of interdependence extend, encompassing the surface of the earth.

But this book is not about the big picture. Our focus is on the intricacies of association between plants and animals and their habitats. In Bates Littlehales' photographs, the background is not just there to make things pretty, but to show us the living habitat of a living thing.

We hope that *Nature's Habitats*, will inspire you to look more closely, to ask questions, to seek greater understanding of the significance of habitats. Why do some kinds of plants and animals live in pine forests and others in hardwood forests? Why is a forest of young trees home to some animals and a forest of old trees home to others? How do habitats influence the plants and animals that live within them? How do plants and animals influence the habitats in which they live? How can a forest be a barrier to a bird and water a barrier to a fish?

Understanding habitat, we become aware of the importance of diversity in our world. A diversity of plants and animals in a habitat means that no predator must rely on only one prey species and that no prey species will be controlled by only one predator. As lines of interdependence become complex webs of interdependence, the strength and stability of the community of plants and animals increases. Conversely, as webs of interdependence are broken down by loss of species through habitat fragmentation and destruction, community and ecosystem stability suffers. These ecological principles are universal. Unfortunately, so are the problems of man's influence on habitats.

When we look with understanding at each tree, each fish, each insect, and each reptile we begin to truly see the forest, the coral reef, the swamp, or the desert. Only then can we appreciate the importance of living diversity to our own existence.

Jerome A. Jackson

(Facing) Perhaps as great a diversity of habitats exists under-water as on land. Although the players on this stage are different, the ecological principles are the same: energy flow begins with the rays of the sun. Below the reach of sunlight, life depends on the infiltration of living and dead edible matter from above. At certain points on the deep ocean floor, fissures venting heat and chemicals support rare life forms such as sea worms.

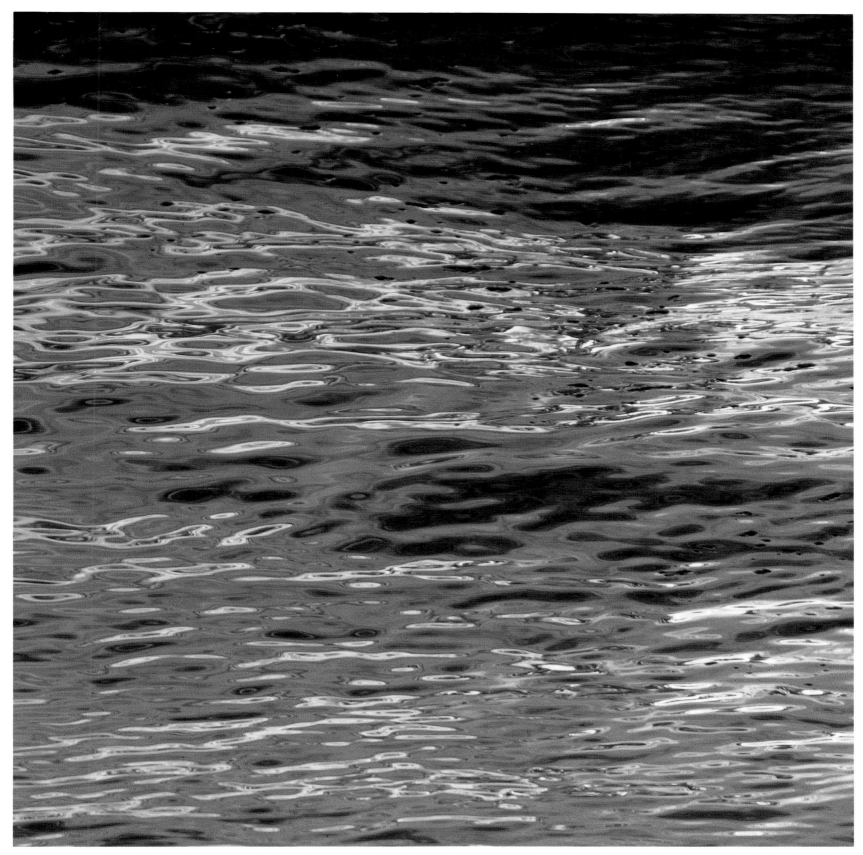

From April to August, tufted puffins, common murres, guillemots, cormorants, and other sea birds find nest sites and safety from predators on the sea stacks and islands of 290-mile-long Oregon Islands NWR. The birds feed on anchovies and other fish in the coast's cold, nutrient-rich seas, an abundance they share with harbor seals and California sea lions.

Water

The most extensive ecosystems on earth are aquatic. Water covers seventy-one percent of the planet's surface, and some ocean trenches in the Pacific exceed six miles in depth. Yet aquatic ecosystems remain largely unknown to us, alien places where we can't exist and where we only visit briefly.

While oceans hold ninety-seven percent of earth's free water, plants and animals find habitat in many other aquatic settings, from trout streams and glacial lakes to desert springs and geothermal pools. An inch of rain in a discarded fifty-gallon drum is all the habitat some larval mosquitos need, and certain tiny frogs in the American tropics spend most of their life cycle in the water that collects between the leaves of bromeliads.

The world's oceans are interconnected, but their depths and shallows, cold and warm waters, and currents and estuaries provide countless byways for species isolation and specialization. As with terrestrial life, each marine creature has unique habitat needs. Waters that do not satisfy those needs are as hostile as prairie to a forest creature.

Aquatic life is most abundant at the oceans' continental fringes, where sunlight reaches vast expanses of shallow water, and algae and aquatic plants flourish. Fish and other free-swimming creatures concentrate around these marine fields and forests, depending on them for food and protective cover. In clear water, adequate light for photosynthesis penetrates a few hundred feet; in muddy water, only fractions of an inch. When topsoil runs into bodies of water from carelessly managed croplands and construction sites, suspended sediments block sunlight, imperiling aquatic habitat vitality.

Cold currents, such as the southward-flowing California current off North America's west coast, mean a richer sea. As cold surface water sinks, warmer waters rise, carrying up microscopic particles of decayed organic material, food for countless planktonic animals and filter-feeding fish, shrimp, and other animals, which then become food for bigger fish, seabirds, and humans.

Living coral reefs are among the most richly populated shallow marine environments and beautifully illustrate species and habitat networks. The photosynthetic, planktonic algae of shallow waters, on which living coral feed, fuel the building of the colony. Coral structures, in turn, partition and diversify the aquatic environment, creating habitat for angelfish, arrow crabs, moray eels, wrasses, and thousands of other animals and plants.

The open ocean is a miles-high blanket of water topped by a thin sheet of algae that sends a sparse rain of dead organic material drifting downward. This organic rain supports a bizarre community in the permanent darkness of deep

(Facing) Thunderstorms and blizzards feed the lakes and marshes of Montana's Red Rock Lakes NWR, habitat for the rare trumpeter swan. Once at home throughout North America, the continent's largest waterfowl survives now in a few refuges in the Rockies and Alaska, where chancy summer weather and aggressive predators often foil nesting attempts. Naturalists fear that the bird may be doomed by dwindling options: limited habitat and a lack of genetic diversity.

The oceans abound with life, but that life is unevenly distributed. Coastal areas, where rivers deposit particulate nutrients from decaying plants and animals, are especially rich. Cold offshore currents also sustain many species; as cold surface water sinks, nutrients rise from the bottom with warmer water. Large schools of fish dot the currents; swimming en masse, like these midwater fingerlings in the Atlantic Ocean, diminishes the chance of being singled out by predators.

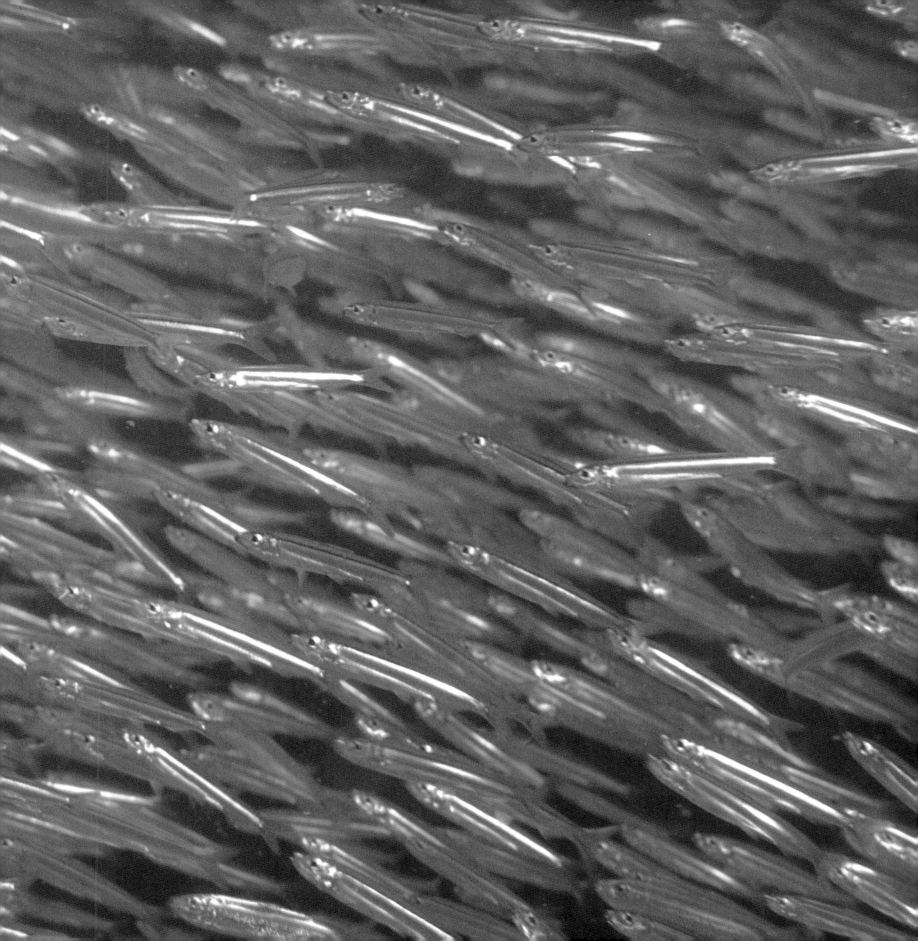

A giant kelpfish waits for prey, hiding amid macrocystis kelp off the California coast. Coastal waters around the world support narrow belts of kelp forest, where—as in terrestrial forests—variations in light and temperature create an abundance of potential niches. Many species of kelp compose these forests. Macrocystis, one of the world's largest plants, sometimes reaches the surface from depths of 260 feet.

ocean habitats. The smallest deep ocean creatures feed by filtering nutrients from the organic rain. Larger creatures prey on them, sometimes with the aid of light-producing or electricity-generating organs.

Even in midocean, currents and upwellings create drift lines of sargassum weed which sustain a following of fishes, crabs, and other animals. Phalaropes and other wide-ranging seabirds seek out the sargassum flotillas, resting on bits of driftwood and feeding on the inhabitants.

Where rivers meet the sea and fresh and salt waters mix, we find some of the world's richest habitats—sounds, estuaries, swamps, and bays which sustain a remarkable spectrum of year-round residents and seasonal migrants. Mississippi Sound, divided from the Gulf of Mexico by a string of barrier islands three to ten miles from the mainland, provides an excellent example.

The islands slow the force of tropical storms, limit the incursion of salt water, and trap silt and organic material from mainland rivers. Riverine sediment makes the sound shallow, and reduced wave action within the island barrier allows marsh vegetation to gain a foothold. These marsh grasses and needle rushes serve two vital filtering functions: thwarting predators by providing inaccessible hiding places for young animals and capturing nutrients washed off land or carried in by tides.

Mississippi Sound's calm, brackish waters and plentiful nutrients create a nursery for marine fishes, crabs, shrimp, and other creatures. Although many of these species live as adults in the Gulf of Mexico, their larvae cannot tolerate its high salinity, and the adults return to the estuary to breed. The resulting concentrations of breeding adults, eggs, and larval sea creatures mean good fishing for humans, marine mammals, and sea, shore, and marsh birds. The largest known concentrations of Atlantic bottle-nosed dolphins feed in the waters of the sound.

The spectrum of habitat use in a place as rich as Mississippi Sound, even by species as closely related as the great blue and green-backed heron and reddish egret, suggests how thoroughly a habitat is partitioned. The great blue heron stands and motionlessly watches for prey in water that would submerge its smaller relatives. The green-backed heron hunts instead from a log or bank, sometimes in the purlieus of very small streams. Not content to watch and wait, this heron may lure its dinner by dropping a feather or leaf on the water as "bait."

The reddish egret is less patient still, often waiting only seconds in one spot before making a wild leap intended to startle prey and flush it out. For its antics to succeed, the reddish egret must have open, shallow water full of prey. Emergent vegetation would simply get in the way.

While marine habitats tend to change little over thousands, even millions of years, freshwater habitats vary ceaselessly—clear today, muddy tomorrow; warm in summer, frozen in winter; turbulent with floods, stagnant with drought; marsh this year, prairie the next. Coping with both seasonal and unpredictable change and finding new habitat when the old disappears are routine requirements for survival.

Airborne plants and animals are often the first to colonize fresh water. The tiny seeds of cattails and willows, wafting along on their silky tufts, inaugurate suitable habitat for hundreds of less mobile aquatic animals. Mosquitos, back-swimmers, diving beetles, dragonflies, and a host of other insects also quickly invade, guaranteeing a food supply for later arrivals.

It's easy to understand that insects in flight perceive new bodies of water. But that doesn't explain the early arrival of frogs, salamanders, and turtles whose eyes are never more than inches above water or land. The answer may lie in a visual ability humans lack. When polarized light strikes a body of water, it rebounds skyward, particularly at dawn and dusk. Some of these animals apparently see this reflected light, learn its direction, then move toward it at night.

If reptiles and amphibians can see the water's reflection in daylight, why don't they travel then? Two clear reasons exist. First, daylight movements increase their exposure to predators. Second, higher daytime temperatures cause them to lose much more body water. Water loss is so hazardous to amphibians that most move only on rainy nights.

The inconstant nature of small ponds and streams compels the animals which breed in them to accurately assess the present and future quality of their habitat. It would be a disaster for frogs to assemble at a small pond and go through courtship and egg-laying, only to have the pond dry up before their tadpoles metamorphosed into adulthood.

For most species, little is left to chance. Inherited behavior patterns, embedded by generations of success against nature's high odds, govern almost every action. One March a few years ago, I attended a meeting in the Catskill Mountains of New York. The snow was melting; I heard wood frogs and decided to see if I could capture some for my natural history class. At a small pool where male wood frogs were calling, I soon grabbed a courting pair. They were already in amplexus, the moment in frog and toad courtship when the male hugs the female from behind and pokes her in the belly with his forelimbs. This stimulates her to deposit her eggs in the water, and the male then releases sperm over them. I put my captives in a plastic gallon pickle jar with about three inches of water, enough, I thought, to hold them until I made it back to Mississippi.

I figured my rude interruption would have disrupted the male wood frog's amour. But three days later, when I arrived in Mississippi, the pair was still in amplexus. Once home, I transferred the two frogs to an aquarium with about five inches of water. Within minutes, the female deposited her eggs, the male released his sperm, and the frogs parted. Was it the shallowness of the water in the jar or the confined area that kept her from releasing her eggs earlier? Whatever the stimulus, they both waited for it.

The gray angelfish hunts during the day along Atlantic and Gulf coast coral reefs. Some, thought to be introduced, also live around Bermuda. Similar habitat conditions foster the fish in both places, but not in the hundreds of miles of ocean between.

(Facing) The northern red anemone, associated with the kelp forests off San Diego, California, takes advantage of the nutrients provided by the upwelling of warmer bottom waters. The anemone's tentacles sway with the current, but when its chemical sensors detect potential food nearby, the tentacles begin waving wildly to pull the food to its open mouth.

(Facing) A goby scavenges among the sedentary residents of a boulder coral colony. Diverse as a mountain in microclimates and topography, a coral reef's surface is habitat for a wide range of creatures. "Living" coral is not itself a creature, but a creature's by-product; each coral-making species builds foundations for its colonies by excreting coral in specific forms.

Habitats in a coral reef are divided by territory, diet, and times of day. This arrow crab hunts at night. Its appearance, slow movements, and careful choice of habitat make it hard to find.

A deft fisherman of southern backwaters, the anhinga swiftly swims underwater after prey which it spears with a spring-like action of special neck muscles. Reaching the surface with a fish impaled on its sharp bill, it jerks its head, flips the fish into the air, and catches it headfirst for ease of swallowing. The anhinga lacks an oil gland to waterproof its feathers and must perch near the water to wait for out-stretched wings to dry.

(Facing) Whooping cranes, among the world's rarest birds, winter in salt marshes at Aransas NWR on Texas' Gulf coast. Similar habitat elsewhere on the Gulf is too polluted, too disturbed, or simply too small. Like trumpeter swans and other big animals which stay together in family groups, whooping cranes need a large contiguous area of habitat to survive.

(Facing) Known for their broad ocean beaches and protected estuaries, the barrier islands of Georgia and the other southeastern states also include interior swamps, formed where rainwater fills sandy depressions. Sealed from the ocean by dunes, rarely broached by hurricane tides, these pools teem with mosquitoes, midges, pig frogs, cottonmouths, and occasional alligators.

A red-shouldered hawk perches in the Florida Everglades. The chief hawk of swampy bottom-land woods, the red-shouldered hawk often watches for prey—frogs, snakes, insects, small mammals—from a well-shaded branch. This individual's relatively pale plumage may reflect the lack of deep shade in its Everglades habitat.

(Facing) Plant habitat is defined by soil type, amount of sunshine, and the quality, quantity, and dependability of water. Dwarf crested iris, a perennial, favors moist sandy or rocky soils in thinly wooded areas of the Southeast. The Smoky Mountain stream-bank where this dew-covered iris blooms is prime habitat for the species.

This false hellebore, flowering in a high-altitude wetland near red spruces in West Virginia's Monongahela National Forest, is one of seven North American species. All grow in cool, moist pastures and open woods. Occasionally called "Indian poke," the poisonous false hellebore is not to be mistaken for the edible (and tasty) pokeweed.

Orb weavers in cold climates are born, mature, and die within a year. In fall, mature spiders deposit an insulated egg case in a sheltered place. Spiderlings emerge in spring and feed and grow through summer. Toward autumn, their webs, which they repair or rebuild every day, become conspicuous. Choosing the right span for the web is crucial in the quest for prey.

(Facing) From late spring to midsummer, male green tree frogs gather each night by southern wooded ponds. Calling out in a barking chorus, they lure the mute females to the pond for mating. By day, they cling to green plants nearby, legs drawn in, head down, concealing themselves from predators and minimizing water loss.

A Virginia mountain stream's splashing current adds oxygen to the water and clears it of silt and loose matter. Fast-water species are specially adapted to live against the current. Some, like trout, have well-developed swimming muscles; others, like the larvae of trout's favored prey, the caddisfly and mayfly, shelter in stone-covered cases glued to the streambed.

*Still water means siltation, a soft bottom, warm temperatures,
and plentiful vegetation—good habitat for herbivorous creatures like
this red-eared slider, an aquatic reptile with neither the muscles
nor the metabolism for fast, cold currents. Basking in the sun and
swimming in warm water speed the turtle's metabolism and
hence its digestion of vegetation.*

(Facing) When a river meets an ocean or large lake, its current slows, releasing its silt load in a broad fan whose marshy shallows are rich in nutrients, vegetation, and habitat for migratory water birds. Rising waters can submerge such a place as the Bear River delta at Utah's Great Salt Lake, driving water birds to other habitat.

In the upper Midwest and the West, the yellow-headed blackbird shares many wetlands with its more familiar red-winged relative. But their proximity depends on carefully partitioned habitat. Yellow-headed blackbirds nest in cattails and other vegetation in water; red-winged blackbirds nest closer to shore.

When beavers, debris, or humans dam woodland streams in places like New York's Montezuma NWR, the flooded trees slowly die. As they decay, a succession of tenants moves in, protected from predators by the water below. First herons, egrets, and other water birds build platform nests in the branches. When dead branches fall, fungi grow in from the scars, softening heartwood. Woodpeckers then excavate cavities, which bluebirds, great crested flycatchers, and others may eventually usurp.

(Facing) Some bottomland hardwoods, such as these oaks and sweet gums near Stuttgart, Arkansas, can withstand—even thrive on—seasonal flooding. Vast flocks of mallards, wood ducks, and other acorn-eating birds once wintered comfortably in these hardwood swamps. Since World War II, however, drainage and levee projects have destroyed vast stretches of this habitat.

Edges

t was getting dark as I worked my way along the mist net, disentangling indigo buntings and putting them in holding bags for banding. I had three birds to go when an excruciating pain shot through my foot. I knew what had happened; I'd stepped on a prickly pear cactus pad and driven its spines through the sole of my sneaker. Jerking backward, I'd pushed other spines through the shoe's side.

My tent, where I had a flashlight and a pair of pliers to extricate the three-inch spines, was a mile away. Before trying to get there, I had to free those birds, or they'd die in the net. Biting my lip, I worked them loose, then spent three hours struggling back to the camp. Every time my left foot touched the sand, I felt more pain as the spines sank deeper into my flesh. Any movement pushes their barbed tips in—a wonderful adaptation for dispersing the cactus pads, which can take root wherever they fall, and a terrible fate for the hapless animal hooked as transport.

I had been alone for three days on East Ship Island in the Gulf of Mexico. I was netting and banding birds to learn about their movements and length of stay. The island is an excellent example of an ecological edge—a place where different habitats meet—and like most edges, it's a good place to find birds.

Here fall migrants make their last stop for food and rest before striking out across the Gulf for wintering areas in the Caribbean and Central America, and returning birds make their first landfall in spring. The arduous Gulf crossing forces these birds to use habitats quite unlike their normal ones. In spring, I've stood on barrier beaches and watched birds skim the waves as they come in, literally tumbling onto dunes in search of food to replenish exhausted reserves. In both fall and spring, any species may turn up in any of the island's habitats: scarlet tanagers chasing grasshoppers across a sand dune, hooded warblers perching like butterflies on saltbush, orchard orioles swinging from sea oat stems.

East Ship Island is part of the edge between North America and the Gulf of Mexico, a meeting ground for species from the mainland and the sea. Many members of barrier island communities are good colonizers—like the prickly pear cactus with its ability to withstand some submersion in salt water and to grab a quick foothold once ashore. Because of its small size, East Ship Island's various habitats are also mostly edges, a patchwork of woods, scrub-covered dunes, freshwater ponds, salt marshes, and grassy meadows bordered by sand beaches. Almost any habitat on the island is within a stone's throw of several others.

Most terrain doesn't bring so many habitats—and therefore edges—together. But wherever edge habitats occur, their plant and animal communities share certain "edge effects": they host species from the pure habitats on either side; they host species peculiar to the edge; and they are places where animals congregate. Whatever

(Facing) On the rocky Channel Islands near Santa Barbara, California, where baking sun alternates with storm tides, few species take hold permanently. Yet a tally of local scavengers and migratory visitors who perch here while searching the waves for food reveals the richness of this edge between marine and terrestrial habitats.

(Facing) *The time during which a species uses a habitat can be very brief, yet very intense. For example, northern elephant seals take over the beaches of California's San Miguel Island for a few weeks in late winter when they breed, and again in the fall when they molt. The rest of the year, the beaches are a temporary stopping place for many species.*

the edge—forest meeting grassland, forest meeting water, grassland meeting agricultural field—the patterns are similar. Only the details and species differ.

The edge effect is undoubtedly strongest where water and land meet. Since all life requires water, all terrestrial animals are drawn to sources of fresh water—even those which spend the rest of their time in other habitats. Moreover, many species of insects, turtles, amphibians, birds, and mammals are more or less at home in both aquatic and terrestrial environments. In the shallow waters of aquatic edges, where emergent vegetation harbors an abundance of small animals above and below the water's surface, wading birds and terrestrial mammals hunt for prey. Along the shore, gulls and other scavengers work the strand lines, where waves and currents have left a rich residue of organic and inorganic matter.

Aquatic edges—especially marine edges—are vital seasonal habitat for many species. Each spring and summer, thousands of sea birds seek to nest on predator-free islets and beaches, especially on the sandy barrier islands of the Atlantic coast and the Gulf of Mexico and the rocky islets and archipelagos of the Pacific coast.

Nowadays, humans also migrate to the beaches in the summer, ruining countless nesting sites with buildings, traffic, and waste. The piping plover, which nests on the Atlantic coast, is endangered, and the least tern has struggled to adapt. Some least terns appear to be making up for lost habitat by taking over the flat gravel rooftops of shopping malls and similar buildings.

Less conspicuous species also need protection. For most of the year, sea turtles live far from shore. But during late June and early July, females land at night on the beaches of the southeast, lay their eggs in the sand, and crawl back to the sea, leaving tracks as wide as a bulldozer's tread. Wind and waves soon wash these away; the eggs remain, buried and vulnerable to humans and predators until they hatch two months later.

At the water's edge, some habitats are themselves seasonal. In much of North America, late summer and early autumn are often dry. Ponds and rivers recede, leaving broad mud flats, edge habitats with a wealth of food for migrant shorebirds: stranded fishes, clams, and snails, swarms of hovering insects, and seedlings sprouting in the mud.

Each species' use of an edge defines that habitat in a different way. To a pair of Canada geese, building their nest at the edge of a prairie marsh in April, that edge is appropriate only in that season, and only for raising young. To the no-see-ums hatching amid the reeds, the shallows at the water's edge and the nearby marsh are the world.

Even within a single species, each sex may occupy an edge habitat—or any habitat—differently. Consider the downy woodpecker, the smallest North American woodpecker, which feeds and nests at forest edges. Males tend to hunt for food on small trees and shrubs and on small branches of large trees, venturing to weedy fields to

extract the larvae of the goldenrod gall fly from their swollen homes along goldenrod stems. Females forage mainly on larger branches and trees at the forest edge. Dividing their habitat, downy woodpeckers may reduce competition for food between the sexes and thus strengthen their pair bond.

Edges' profoundly linear form makes them places of movement and transition. Where a forest or lake might be a polygon or an ellipse, enclosing species, an edge is always a line, a border, a thin zone or corridor between broad zones. For this reason, many species travel along edge habitats. Shorelines, for example, often include a fringe of bare beach, mud, or rock where erratic or extreme changes in water level and turbulence keep plants from taking hold. These bare areas are inviting pathways: no underbrush slows movements, visibility is good, and the protective cover of water or vegetation isn't far away.

Often, species disperse widely along shorelines and other edge habitats. Aquatic, amphibious, and shoreline colonizers spread inland along rivers and streams to their sources. Along the rivers of the Great Plains, cottonwoods and willows convey plants and animals from the forests and forest edges of eastern North America to islands of trees in prairie towns and windbreaks along farm boundaries.

Habitat edges are often marked by changing air currents—pathways for many birds. At the seashore, gulls, terns, ospreys, and other birds ride the almost continual breezes generated by the differing temperatures of land and sea. Over grasslands and near cliff faces and mountainsides, hawks, vultures, eagles, storks, and other soaring birds exploit rising air currents to hunt or travel. When mountain ridges run more or less north-south, associated thermals become major migratory pathways.

While we've blithely destroyed many edge habitats, we've inadvertently created others. Twentieth-century highway construction has created new corridors for species dispersal. Weeds prosper in disturbed areas—and what is more disturbed than a highway right-of-way? Queen Anne's lace, showy evening primrose, and bitterweed and other yellow composite flowers thrive at the edge of highways, their seeds sometimes dispersed by passing traffic.

Amid the grasses and low vegetation that edge highways, cotton rats and other rodents find prime habitat. Drawn by their presence, hawks and owls perch and nest in adjacent forest edges. Recently, along some highways in the southeast where pines have been planted, a much rarer bird has appeared—the red-cockaded woodpecker. Once at home in the now-vanishing mature southeastern pine forest, the red-cockaded woodpecker favors open areas, often excavating its nest and roost cavities on forest edges. Some now appear to find the same open conditions on highway rights-of-way. And not long ago, a banded red-cockaded woodpecker was found to have moved nearly sixty miles between two colonies along the same North Carolina highway.

(Facing) Habitat is often austere where land and sea meet. California's northern coast is buffeted by salty winds, generated by differing sea and land temperatures. Waves eat at the rocky cliffs, and steep slopes frequently crumble. Like grasses on sand dunes, the probing roots of dudleya and other plants help stabilize the shoreline.

*S*ea gull? There's no such animal. "Shore gull" would be a better name; these ubiquitous coastal creatures rarely fly out of sight of land. On fresh or salt water, on oceans, lakes, or rivers, the meeting of water and land provides a continual bounty of flotsam for these scavengers to inspect and consume.

For tufted puffins at California's Farallon Islands NWR,
the edge between rock and ocean is hospitable. Nutrients brought to
the surface by the cold Pacific current mean an abundance of fish,
and the predator-free islands provide sites for nest burrows.

Driftwood at Point Lobos, California, bridges marine and terrestrial habitats. Drift-wood can also serve as a focus for a resident community of crabs, insects, isopods, and plants. The flow of wind and water is blocked, sand accumu-lates, seeds germinate: the land reaches out, if only temporarily.

*The sea also reaches in, eroding sand, soil, and rock.
At Ossabaw Island, Georgia, and other southeastern
barrier islands, the current washes away the outer shore,
swallowing forests. But the islands persist because eddies
deposit sand in calm waters at one end, creating new
land. In coastal environments, change is the rule,
but life continues.*

*E*dges sometimes mark the limit of the dispersal of plants and animals. This photograph appears to illustrate a single habitat: deciduous forest. But habitats must be viewed from each species' perspective. To a white-tailed deer, this is one habitat. But to a land snail, the little brook, a hostile habitat, permanently divides two favorable zones.

(Facing) The white-throated sparrow, a ground feeder, lives on seeds. When snow blankets its nesting range for too long, concealing potential food, this sparrow migrates to similar but warmer habitat nearby—a pattern followed by other ground feeders. In recent years, bird feeders have enticed many ground-feeding birds to winter in their snowbound nesting habitat.

Sequences of habitats often follow predictable patterns. Altitude and temperature dictate a mountain's progression of habitats, and a river's current is sure to disperse streamside vegetation and small animals downstream. Some of the plants in this Potomac River wetland were carried in by floods, which left behind seeds and even living trees and shrubs.

(Facing) An oxbow lake in an alluvial forest in Maryland shelters mallards, a duck species which lives in a broad range of habitats. Within woodlands, ponds create small patches of a second habitat surrounded by a fertile border zone. Some, like this oxbow lake, form when a river changes course; others appear when beavers dam a stream.

(Facing) Rhododendrons and other heath shrubs cloak Appalachian heath balds, growing too densely for tree seedlings to sprout. If "natural" heath balds exist, they begin with fires ignited by lightning. In West Virginia's Dolly Sods Wilderness Area, the heaths began with logging and subsequent fires.

In summer, the magnolia warbler lives in Canada's vast spruce-fir forests. On spring and fall migrations, the species visits forest edges in the United States, where it finds water and an abundance of insects. John James Audubon, who first spotted migrating magnolia warblers in a Mississippi magnolia tree, is responsible for the misleading name.

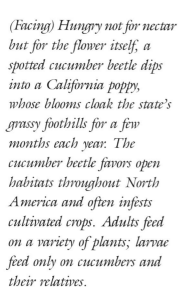

(Facing) Hungry not for nectar but for the flower itself, a spotted cucumber beetle dips into a California poppy, whose blooms cloak the state's grassy foothills for a few months each year. The cucumber beetle favors open habitats throughout North America and often infests cultivated crops. Adults feed on a variety of plants; larvae feed only on cucumbers and their relatives.

Bumblebees and honeybees enrich the edge between forest and field, pollinating the grasslands' annuals and perennials as well as many forest plants. In many areas, bumblebees are the main pollinators of the first spring flowers. The ability to regulate their body temperatures allows them to be active on cooler days and for longer periods than honeybees.

A courting male blue grouse displays near a forest's edge in Montana's National Bison Range. Blue grouse haunt edges and are seldom found deep within the forest or far from trees. They nest and summer in open, brushy thickets, feeding on berries. When danger approaches, the whir of wings from a sentry sends the grouse to safety in nearby trees.

(Facing) In many habitats, rock outcrops begin as sterile openings. Then wind, rain, heat, and cold gradually erode and fracture the rock. Lichens, among the first organisms to pioneer bare rock, mix organic matter with eroded mineral grains to produce a pittance of soil in a fracture line—perhaps enough to allow a single seed to germinate.

Forests

N ow what are you going to do?"

Three thousand feet up and three miles from the airport, my instructor reached over and reduced the power, simulating a dead engine. I'd been waiting for this moment. I was taking my last lesson before my flight exam with the FAA, and I'd heard that instructors sometimes tested their students in this way.

I put the plane in a glide path that would set me down a hundred yards beyond the runway threshold. Like a bullet in slow motion, the Cessna glided toward my target. We were over a pasture, it was a late summer afternoon, and it was eerily pleasant to hear the wind instead of the engine.

A mile from the runway, I was at 1,200 feet. A three-quarter-mile long patch of woods lay ahead. Suddenly, my plane began to sink rapidly. I couldn't maintain my glide path. The altimeter plummeted—800, 700, 550 feet.

I pushed in the throttle and the engine coughed and roared to life. After gaining some altitude, I managed to come in for one of my better landings. What a lesson! I'll never forget it.

Bare ground, grass, rock, and concrete reflect a tremendous amount of heat. That reflected heat provides lift, and that's what was carrying me toward the runway. A forest, on the other hand, absorbs heat—no upward currents, no lift.

As a biologist, I have often pondered this lesson. Before Europeans arrived, most of eastern North America was heat-absorbing forest. Today, much of it is heat-reflecting farmland or urban sprawl. For vultures and the larger hawks, things have improved. More heat-reflecting land means more habitat, more thermals to ride as they hunt or migrate.

Other animals haven't benefited. A once-continuous forest has been fragmented into ribbons along waterways and patches between fields and buildings. The extensive habitat required by the eastern cougar and the ivory-billed woodpecker is all but gone.

Before my experience in the Cessna, I'd known how the destruction of the eastern forest had severely disrupted individual species and habitat communities, but I hadn't thought about the effect on the climate.

A forest, even a small stand of trees, moderates extremes of weather—witness the shelter belts midwestern farmers plant on the north and west edges of their land. Within a forest, the leafy canopy buffers winter wind and summer sun. Resilient, leathery leaves dampen the force of a hard rain and relay each drop downward.

Forests protect watersheds. Because shade makes a forest cooler than other environments, water evaporates more slowly, making the microclimate more humid. Snow and ice remain longer in forests, gradually distributing moisture to streams, ponds, and soil. Forest soils also retain water, releasing it more slowly and steadily,

(Facing) Great Smoky Mountains National Park exemplifies the concept that habitat diversity promotes species diversity. High rainfall, great elevational differences, isolated areas, and a geographic position between North America's coastal plain and interior combine to give this park more tree species than all of Europe.

with less silt, than many other environments.

Forests can serve as barriers between other habitats, slowing the diffusion of harmful nonforest insects and diseases borne by nonforest species. Some nonforest species also use woodlands as corridors between habitats. The gray *Myotis* bat, for example, flies through the forest from cave shelters to feeding areas along wooded streams.

Just as the forest's influence on the environment varies with acreage, maturity, predominant tree species, and placement among other habitats, its attractiveness to possible inhabitants depends on many variables. Even a single tree can provide habitat for some forest organisms. A sustainable population of land snails might find sufficient forest habitat in three wooded acres. A single pair of hairy woodpeckers—hardly a sustainable population—needs thirty acres. How many pairs of woodpeckers are needed to prevent the species from sliding into oblivion? Must their forest habitat be continuous? These are the questions facing conservation biologists. For some species, the answers will determine survival or extinction.

Species differ greatly in their tolerance for variety. The great horned owl will inhabit almost any forest where food is available. The endangered spotted owl of the Pacific Northwest requires forest of a certain minimum acreage and maturity. Amphibians depend on the moisture regime—patterns of rainfall and humidity— and on reliable springs, ponds, and streams. Forest plants need specific soil structures and pH, amounts of sun or shade, and patterns of fire and flooding.

By clearing forests, we've altered an untold number of ecological networks, patterns, and pathways in North America. We also affect remaining woodlands, where management and controlled growth modify networks of diversity and interdependence. A few key points in that network help illustrate the perils of human forest management.

Tree growth in a forest is highly competitive. Leaves are trees' power plants, driving their growth by photosynthesizing sunlight into simple sugars. Each tree reaches toward sunlight, pushing its canopy of leaves above its neighbors', growing straight and tall.

A tree in an open field doesn't compete for sunlight. Energy goes into lateral growth, producing a broad root system and a short, stout shape whose wide shade area discourages competitors. A tall, slender forest tree, sheltered from wind, surrounded by competitors, needs a smaller "footprint" of roots securing it. When woodcutters remove most of the forest and leave only scattered trees, the remaining trees often snap off or blow over.

Forest tree species influence how water reaches the community beneath them. Northern conifers' downward- and outward-stretching limbs send snow sliding off, preventing branches from breaking. In waterlogged soils, the same structure channels rain to the tips of the branches, keeping the tree's base drier than the periphery. By contrast, when trees have upward-reaching branches—like many in arid environments—rain flows down the branches and trunk and waters the base and roots.

(Facing) Great horned owls thrive in many habitats and live in forests throughout the Americas. Formidable predators, they capture mammals as large as house cats, rabbits, and skunks. To lay their eggs, they usurp old nests of red-tailed hawks, other large birds, and squirrels. They also nest on cliffs, and even building ledges, if nothing harasses them and prey is available nearby.

(Facing) Conifer forests on dry slopes sometimes appear to be held in the grip of fingers of aspen forest, reaching along moist ravines from rivers. And in some ways, aspens do hold them. Resinous conifers quickly carry wildfires, while the aspens' wetter habitat defuses them. Ravaging insects, which are often very host-specific, can also be slowed by aspen barriers.

(Page 64) Some view West Virginia's species-rich Monongahela National Forest as an inefficient source of timber. But this view overlooks the forest's true riches. In diversity is stability; with monoculture, disaster from insects or disease always looms.

These differences in form vary not only with species, but with age. Young trees often have more upward-reaching branches than mature trees. In a diverse, mature forest, these variations create a mosaic of microhabitats at ground level. Some modern forest management—harvesting by clear-cutting, planting one lucrative species instead of encouraging the local mix—changes distribution patterns and the communities that depend on them.

When trees mature, their load of dead wood multiplies; new growth, reaching skyward, kills older limbs by blocking their light. Although leaves and living tissues support many living things, the forest community literally mushrooms as dead wood increases. When decayed limbs break off, wood-boring insects and wood-rotting fungi invade the scars and stubs. As the heartwood softens, woodpeckers excavate nests. Fungi also create natural cavities, soon occupied by an array of birds, squirrels, mice, lizards, snakes, and bees. If cavities collect rainwater, they may become homes for tree frogs or watering holes for many species.

Littering the forest floor, dead limbs and leaves create another tier of habitat and contribute to the soil's chemistry and fertility. They also make the forest more easily combustible.

Over time, we've learned how fire contributes to many forest dwellers' survival. Before Europeans arrived here, a lightning-caused fire might burn for hundreds of miles. Roads, communities, and farmlands now block the spread of natural blazes. And those that do get started are usually quickly put out. As a result, a perilous fuel load of dead leaves, needles, and limbs has increased year after year, and fires nowadays can rapidly become very destructive. More frequent fires that reduce the fuel load would be better for the forest.

In the southeastern United States, there are more electrical storms than anywhere else in North America—in central Florida, they strike roughly ninety days per year. By necessity, southeastern plants and animals coexist with fire. Consider the longleaf pine. Its needles occur in bundles of three and are as much as a foot long. Falling to the ground, they collect in small, tepee-shaped piles. When bundle after bundle of needles falls, the ground litter becomes a loose duff with lots of trapped air. Fires race through, doing little damage to fire-adapted species.

Southern pines, in fact, need fire. In shade, their seeds may germinate, but seedlings will die. By producing a loose litter of highly flammable needles, the pines encourage fire, controlling competition and creating a habitat in which their seedlings can grow.

The animals of the southern pine forests are also fire-adapted. The gopher tortoise, diamondback rattlesnake, dusky gopher frog, and others take refuge in the tortoise's burrows. The gray rat snake has become arboreal and seeks shelter in tree cavities. Like the species that make up any forest community, their relation to their habitat is very precise.

(Right) "Hearts-a-bustin" is a Tennessee nickname for American burning bush, a native of the deciduous forests of the Smoky Mountains. The shrub shows little color until fall, when its seed capsules split open to reveal a brilliant reddish orange center.

(Below) The angle-wing katydid is one of nature's masters of deception. Supporting wing veins mimic the supportive conduits of leaves in its deciduous forest home. To speed its feeding, a katydid will often hold the leaf it's eating in its front legs.

A cool, moist, shaded area with a slightly acid soil, such as this Tennessee mixed hardwood and pine forest, provides habitat for twinberry or partridgeberry. Both names are meaningful. The white to pink flowers and peppermint-tasting berries occur in pairs on this inch-high plant, and in winter, partridge, grouse, and other birds eat the berries, as do foxes, skunks, and mice.

(Facing) The cleft-foot amanita, growing here on West Virginia's Elk Mountain, is common throughout hardwood and mixed forests in eastern North America. Amanitas are among the world's most poisonous mushrooms to humans. All emerge from a fleshy cuplike volva at the base, and have white gills and spores and a stem encircled by a fleshy annulus where the opening cap breaks free.

The mountain dusky sala-
mander, a nocturnal forager
whose color varies tremen-
dously, strays far from water
during the summer, but
returns to springs and seeps in
winter. The rugged geology of
the southern Appalachians
isolates salamanders, leading
to more species variety in this
moist woodland habitat than
any other place in the world.

(Facing) Lichens are impor-
tant decomposers or recyclers
in forest ecosystems. This
slow-growing, long-lived
lichen, called the brown-
fruited cup cladonia, goblet
lichen, or pixie cup, grows on
stumps and in rich soil,
favoring mosses on barren
southeastern slopes of mixed
eastern forests. Trapping
moisture, pixie cup creates a
microhabitat for other
organisms on the forest floor.

(Facing) Xeromphalina
mushrooms such as this
cluster in West Virginia grow
on well-rotted hardwood
stumps and logs. When a
complete Xeromphalina spec-
imen is dried, it has the rare
ability to revive if placed in
water—a useful adaptation in
its high woodland habitat,
which alternates between
wet and dry.

*Mature male eastern box
turtles have red eyes; the eyes
of females and the young are
yellow. At home in deciduous
forests dotted with tree-fall
clearings where berries grow,
the omnivorous, land-dwelling
box turtle will snap up ripe
strawberries, blackberries,
fleshy mushrooms, or insects
and spiders. The elusive hatch-
lings, which emerge in
September, feed on earth-
worms and beetle larvae
under rotting logs.*

The gray Myotis *bat, found in lower midwestern and south central states, relies on three separate habitats: caves, forests, and streams and lakes. It hibernates and raises young in caves and commutes through the shelter of forests to waters where it feeds on insects. Today, this* Myotis *is endangered. Amateur cavers frequently disturb its caves. And when clear-cutting takes out the forest between a cave and feeding waters, the gray* Myotis *often abandons that entire region.*

(Facing) When autumn arrives in Shenandoah National Park and other deciduous forests, habitat changes, and so does the resident community. As leaves die and fall, leaf-feeding insects either fast and hibernate or leave eggs that will survive the winter. Insect-eating birds make a seasonal shift in diet or migrate to habitat where insects are still active.

The southern flying squirrel, active at night, eats the same acorns as tree squirrels. But this squirrel not much larger than a big hamster can hang glide by stretching taut the loose folds of skin between front and hind legs. Its habitat requirements include a supply of nuts, buds, and insects for food, old woodpecker holes or natural cavities for safe sleeping and nesting, and open forest for easy gliding.

(Facing) Some trees will die in this Oregon forest fire. But the fire will also return essential minerals to the soil, prepare openings for germination of seedlings, and stimulate cones to release their seeds. When fires are suppressed for many years, truly devastating blazes become likely as needles, twigs, and branches pile up on the forest floor.

The understated plumage of this female spruce grouse suits her Maine habitat. Spruce grouse inhabit the north woods from the Atlantic to the Pacific, requiring extensive stands of cool spruce forest interspersed with bogs, swamps, or small clearings. During the winter, they feed extensively on spruce buds and needles. In other seasons, their diet is more varied.

(Facing) Trees are shaped by their environment—and shape it. Exposed to constant wind during its life, this Monterey cypress at Point Lobos, California, developed strong, short boughs. Growing in the open, it expanded outward. Had neighbors surrounded it, their shapes would have influenced the twists and turns of its branches.

In the pine and oak savannahs of the California foothills, California ground squirrels go aloft each spring to feed on the oak's tiny green acorns. Climbing through the outer branches, the squirrels knock many acorns to the ground. Amid a superabundance of food, they nibble a bit, remove the hull, and drop the unfinished nut, which California quail and other ground-foraging birds readily devour.

Deserts

When we think of deserts, we often think of very hot places: the Sahel, Death Valley, the Mojave Desert. But heat alone does not create a desert. Mongolia's Gobi Desert and Wyoming's Great Divide Basin are bitterly cold in winter and only moderately warm in summer.

Hot or cold, most deserts share one feature: minimal precipitation. Scientific definitions of deserts vary, but all agree that desert conditions prevail where precipitation totals less than ten or fifteen inches a year. Vegetation is another measure; in desert habitat, plants cover less than fifty percent of the ground.

Why is desert precipitation so scanty? The answer lies in physical laws and geographical circumstances which cause the atmosphere to acquire and distribute moisture unevenly. Earth's equatorial regions receive sunlight more directly and warm up more than polar regions. Oceans cover many equatorial regions, and since water's rate of evaporation increases with heat, surface water evaporates rapidly in the heated air.

Like all heated gases, warm, moist air rises. As it does, cooler air from north and south of the equator sweeps in beneath it, creating the air currents known as the trade winds.

Rising, the air cools off, and the earth's rotation deflects it north and south. As it cools, its moisture condenses and falls as rain, mostly within the tropics, where many of the world's rain forests grow.

While warm air rises, cool, dry air falls, warming up in the process and absorbing water from the land through evaporation. Dry, cool air that has been deflected from the equatorial regions descends and dries out the land at latitudes about thirty degrees north and south of the equator.

A glance at a globe shows the result: the Saharan, Arabian, Iranian, Turkestani, and North American deserts extend from the thirtieth degree north of the equator, and Africa's Namib and the deserts of Australia and South America cross the thirtieth degree southward. Most of the world's deserts straddle these latitudes.

Deserts also develop on the leeward side of mountain ranges. As wind blows up a mountain slope, it cools and its moisture condenses, falling as rain or snow which often sustains a lush forest habitat. Sweeping down the leeward slope, dried-out air warms, causes moisture in the terrain to evaporate, and creates desert conditions. The higher the mountain, the greater this effect.

These deserts are said to be in the "rain shadow" of the mountains. The cool deserts of the American Great Basin are typical rain shadow deserts. Some of the world's most extreme deserts—Death Valley, for example—are in rain shadows at a latitude of thirty degrees or so.

(Facing) The saguaro bespeaks the desert Southwest. In fact, the huge cactus' range is limited to southern Arizona, southeastern California, and northern Mexico. Slow-growing and highly susceptible to human disturbances, saguaros require rocky or gravelly soil to anchor their roots. In the right conditions, the desert plant will grow as high as 50 feet, live up to 250 years, and weigh as much as 12 tons.

The term "desert" also covers any sparsely vegetated area. Wave action keeps vegetation from beaches, which are called "coastal deserts." Rock slides and talus slopes are "moving deserts" where the constant shifting of rock prevents plants from gaining a foothold. "Rock deserts" lack soil in which plants can take root. Alpine and tundra areas can be "cold deserts" if frequent or permanent snow and ice restrict plants. Even parking lots have an official name—"cultural deserts."

The desert's sparse vegetation sharply limits the diversity of animal life. Limited diversity means that desert species tend to be highly dependent on one another. Two giants of the desert world, the saguaro and the joshua tree, provide examples. The world's largest cactus, the saguaro grows in the Sonoran Desert of Mexico, Arizona, and California, reaching heights of fifty feet and more. For the gila woodpecker and the gilded flicker, the saguaro is the only desert plant large enough to accommodate their nest cavities. Flycatchers, small owls, bluebirds, and others depend not only on the saguaro to provide a nest site, but also on the woodpeckers to excavate cavities for their desert homes.

Saguaros and joshua trees grow slowly and live a long time—saguaros as long as 250 years, joshua trees for many centuries. Some are said to be thousands of years old, an estimate which can't be proven because the joshua tree, a member of the lily family, doesn't have a true tree's growth rings.

These plants' longevity stabilizes habitat for the creatures that depend on them. Unfortunately, their slow growth also means that damaged habitats will not soon recover. In minutes, an off-road vehicle can mar desert areas that will take centuries to recover. And saguaros are seriously threatened by "cactus-nappers" who find a ready market for their victims in desert suburbia.

Responding to the desert's seasonal extremes, plants flower and animals breed in precisely regulated rhythms which capitalize on periods of higher moisture and lower temperatures. Many desert plants are annuals, living their entire lives during more favorable months and leaving only their seeds to outlast the hottest, driest months.

Elk in Montana's Missouri Brakes, bighorn sheep in the Sonoran Desert, and other large desert grazers and browsers follow seasonal routes to higher and lower elevations, timing their movements to make the most of plant growth. In a sense, they are tracking their prey.

Daily extremes of desert weather also dictate when blossoms open and animals are active. The desert is "alive" from dusk until dawn. By midmorning, many flowers close and most animals retreat to burrows or crevices to minimize water loss.

Many desert species have developed fascinating structural and physiological adaptations to their harsh environment. While helping the species that possesses them, these adaptations frequently present obstacles to others. The extensive root systems that help desert plants gather water efficiently also limit competition by releasing chemicals into the soil that inhibit the growth of other plants. A chemical inhibi-

(Facing) The white-winged dove is a familiar bird of the southwest desert, migrating there to breed. Announcing their presence with continuous cooing, these doves nest in riverside willows, sycamores, and oaks, in mesquite thickets, and sometimes in cholla cactus. Occasionally they feed on cactus fruits.

(Facing) Kofa NWR in Arizona encompasses jagged mountain peaks and hidden canyons. Within the refuge, elevation differences of more than 2,000 feet increase habitat and species diversity.

The horned lizard often positions itself beside a column of ants and casually flicks each passerby into its mouth. Although the lizard withstands 100-degree temperatures, on hot days it burrows to cooler levels of soft soil or sand.

tor accounts for the uniform, wide spacing of creosote bushes.

The creosote bush derives its name from a resinous leaf coating which smells like the wood preservative and limits water evaporation from leaf surfaces. Most desert plants produce similar waxy coatings. Plants of the palo verde group take a further step to save water by dropping their leaves during heat and drought. The photosynthesis they need to survive continues at a minimal level in the green bark of their twigs.

Because plants lose water when animals eat their leaves, desert trees and shrubs must present a discouraging prospect for browsers—thorns, spines, an unpleasant taste, a trace of poison. The spines with which cacti defend their stores of water coincidentally benefit the cactus wren, for whom the sharp barriers mean well-protected nest sites.

Some creatures seem preadapted to the water problem. Insects' and spiders' hard exoskeletons minimize water loss through evaporation, as do the exoskeletons of scorpions and the scales of reptiles. Reptiles and birds excrete body wastes as uric acid, a semisolid white paste which uses very little water. Mammalian urea is far more toxic and must be diluted.

Other creatures have changed. As in every habitat, adaptive flexibility contributes largely to a species' survival and potential range, a point which was brought home to me a few years ago in Wyoming's sagebrush country.

We were conducting a bird survey on land about to be mined for coal. I became especially interested in the western meadowlark after finding six meadowlark nests in exactly the same kind of site. Elsewhere, I've found meadowlark nests concealed in clumps of grass. Here, where expanses of native grass are uncommon, each nesting meadowlark had selected the center of a flat clump of prickly pear cactus. Having felt the pain a prickly pear can inflict, I can't imagine a safer site.

We also surveyed the sage sparrow, a sagebrush resident which almost always places its nest under that shrub and shows little aptitude for change. Next to our sagebrush area lay country that had already been mined. Obligated by law to revegetate, the coal company did so in the most expedient way, planting a hardy grass from desert South Africa. It grows very well in central Wyoming. Local ranchers' cattle will thrive on it, no doubt. But habitat for many native species has been completely—perhaps permanently—altered. Meadowlarks may find places to nest in this African grass, but sage sparrows won't give it another look. Their days in the region will pass with the sagebrush.

(Facing) An intricate maze of canyons, caves, dry washes, and occasional hidden springs surround a rugged upthrust in Kofa NWR. The rocks create patches of welcome shade for the animals which live in this arid landscape. In some of the narrow canyons, which are shaded much of the time, unusual plants like the native fan palm cling to life.

The Mojave diamond rattlesnake grows up to four feet long and preys rapaciously on ground squirrels, kangaroo rats, and pocket mice. Often found in grassy areas where its rodent prey eat seeds, the diamond rattler shelters from searing desert noons in rodent burrows and beneath mesquite and creosote bushes. Its range extends from the Mojave Desert east into Texas and south into Mexico.

(Facing) At the instigation of the Boy Scouts of America, Arizona's Cabeza Prieta NWR was established in 1939 to protect the desert bighorn sheep. The bighorn shares the refuge with the very rare Sonoran pronghorn and many desert animals whose range barely extends into the United States from Mexico.

A gila monster reveals its poisonous lower jaw in Cabeza Prieta NWR. The gila monster and the closely related beaded lizard of western Mexico are the world's only poisonous lizards. The gila monster hunts rodents and other small animals; lacking the specialized teeth of poisonous snakes, it grips its prey in its jaws and slowly works in the venom.

At the tips of the saguaro's limbs, white blooms and a melonlike fragrance attract pollinating birds, insects, and bats. Saguaros bloom in May and produce red fruits in June. White-winged doves, white-throated wood rats, and others eat the fruits and seeds. Less hardy than adults, young saguaros need the shade of ground vegetation, which livestock overgrazing sometimes destroys.

(Facing) Gila woodpeckers and northern (gilded) flickers excavate nest and roost cavities in the saguaro's fluted arms and trunks. To seal the wound, the saguaro lines the cavity with a corky substance, which makes it a valuable bird roost for many years. When a saguaro is lost in a particular habitat, its tenants—ferruginous pygmy-owls, elf owls, ash-throated fly-catchers, and brown-crested flycatchers— also disappear.

Little life appears on vast rocky stretches of the plateaus, cliffs, and slopes of Utah's Zion National Park. Terrific heat and dryness bar most plant pioneers from the terrain, and occasional torrential rains wash away the tiny pockets of eroded silt that any pioneer needs for a foothold. Here and there, a single pine or juniper finds a crevice where enough soil has accumulated to give it a start.

Sandstone towers at Utah's Arches National Park seem to support little life. Nonetheless, some creatures find habitat advantages here. As bare rock reflects the sun's heat, nearby air heats up. Slight breezes enhance its skyward movement, creating thermal updrafts. Riding the thermals, turkey vultures, hawks, ravens, and other aerial predators save energy on hunting flights. To them, caves and ledges in the rock faces are premium roost and nest sites.

Eroding from sandstone spires in Arches National Park, accumulated sand creates a foothold for saltbush. In turn, desert insects feed on the salt bush, and lizards and birds seek out those insects. Deer also browse heavily on saltbush, and their feces support other creatures and contribute to pockets of more fertile soil. From these simple beginnings come habitat complexity and species interdependence.

Gambel's quail inhabits brushy drains and canyons in much of the Southwest. Areas dominated by mesquite, yucca, prickly pear, and sagebrush all suit this quail, which can eat almost any available seeds or succulent leaves.

Round-tailed ground squirrels survive in the Arizona desert by virtue of their burrows, where they spend the hottest part of the day, conserving body water and staying cool. On a day when the desert air is 104 degrees and the soil surface is 165 degrees, the temperature within the burrow remains below 85.

The desert's sun-warmed rocks and sand energize desert reptiles, increasing their rate of metabolism and ability to move quickly to capture prey. The range of thermal safety is narrow, however, and at midday, reptiles seek shelter from the sun. Early evening, while the rocks and sand are still warm, is a prime hunting time.

Hidden recesses of the arid Missouri Brakes in Montana provide habitat for elk—the wapiti of the Shawnee. Most active around dawn and dusk, family groups of two dozen or more graze on grasses, herbaceous plants, and twigs and bark, moving up the mountains in spring and descending in the fall. In early fall, the cliffs and mesas echo with the bugling calls of the bulls.

The cactus wren, a conspicuous resident of southwestern scrublands and deserts, only appears where cactus or thorny shrubs are available as nesting sites. Their flask-shaped grass nests are equally visible. Each pair usually uses two nests at a time, one for nesting and the other for roosting.

(Facing) Palo verde means "green stick," a name bestowed by Spanish explorers on several woody plants of the Southwest. Plants grow when their leaves manufacture sugars through photosynthesis. But in the desert, water evaporates extremely rapidly through leaf surfaces. The various palo verde plants compromise with green photosynthetic cells in their twigs' bark. When water is scarce, they drop their leaves, and photosynthesis in the twigs keeps their metabolic rate above the threshold of survival.

Grasslands

When I was a graduate student at the University of Kansas, a spring ritual practiced by many rural Kansans intrigued me. "Burn the prairie," they declared. "It improves the forage for cattle."

One fall, I was too busy to mow the grass, and my yard became a miniprairie. By February, a few green blades showed beneath tall tufts of dried grasses. I thought, why not burn off the yard as farmers do their pastures? A simple fire would remove the dead grasses, fertilize the lawn, and make the garden easier to till.

It took only one match to set the grass afire and only fifteen seconds to realize I'd made a dreadful mistake. A line of fire raced for my house, and the outdoor faucets were still turned off to keep them from freezing.

"Bring the buckets!" I yelled. And I began beating the flames with my jacket.

Ten minutes later, my yard was scorched and I was covered with soot, but I'd managed to keep the fire from the house. The same weekend, a friend tried the same weed-control technique and burned down a neighbor's garage.

Within days, my lawn was green with new growth. That's the nature of prairie grasses. Like southern pines and other fire-climax plants, they thrive in an environment that burns periodically.

Among grasses' dry, narrow blades, fires start and travel quickly, removing dead material that shades new shoots, killing competitors, and leaving a layer of ashes rich with minerals. An extensive, nutrient-storing root system, punctuated by an abundance of nodes where new shoots will emerge, enables grasses to rebound quickly.

Burning does not insure a grassland habitat. Patterns of grassland vegetation depend on interactions between fire, temperature, precipitation, soil conditions, and other factors. The Great Plains of North America exemplify how grassland habitats vary. In their natural state, the eastern edges are savanna—grassland with scattered trees. To the west, pressured by too much fire and not enough precipitation, trees yield entirely to tall-grass prairie, which yields in turn to short-grass prairie as precipitation declines farther west. In the foothills of the Rockies, cooler temperatures and increased moisture once again encourage savanna and forest.

Like the world's other grasslands, the Great Plains has been habitat to many species of grazing mammals from bison and pronghorns to domestic cattle. Over the millennia, grasses with characteristics that resist grazing have evolved. The tissues of prairie grasses incorporate silicon dioxide—the substance of sand—which quickly wears down mammal teeth. In response, bison have developed teeth which grow constantly and are shaped to grind tough tissues. Adaptation and coadaptation, the dynamic balance that inexorably brings change, fine-tunes the relationships of plants and animals, predators and prey, of each creature and its physical environment.

(Facing) Goldenrod's bright flowers attract the buckeye butterfly and many other insects whose interest is rewarded with nectar or pollen. Blooming in late summer, goldenrod and ragweed, an associated grassland flower, mean hay fever to many. But it is the abundant small pollen grains of the ragweed that bring on hay fever. Relying on wind, ragweed puts its energy into an abundance of lightweight pollen; its flowers are small and inconspicuous. Relying on insects, goldenrod makes less pollen and bigger, more alluring flowers.

Unlike forest creatures, grassland animals can't easily conceal themselves among tall trees and vegetation. Some have adapted with disruptive coloration, earth colors broken by bold white, brown, or black patterns that interrupt body outlines. In a zoo, a pronghorn's patterns are eye-catching. A hundred yards away on the prairie, you may not see the pronghorn at all.

When an ecosystem changes suddenly, species have no time to adapt. Change came rapidly to the American prairies when nineteenth-century settlers discovered how fertile the soil was. A sponge-like mat, the extensive roots of grasses decay into a rich, black soil or sod so firm that early settlers cut it into blocks and built houses with it. Put to the plow, the soil is unsurpassable for growing wheat, corn, and other crops—if it rains enough.

While adult insects and their larvae may share the same general habitat, their micro-habitats are worlds apart—so much so that they often have different predators, feed on different things, have different modes of locomotion, and are affected differently by weather conditions. This cecropia moth has just left its silken cocoon and the bushes it was restricted to as a caterpillar to take to the air in search of a mate.

There's precious little natural prairie left on the Great Plains today, and as it has vanished, so have many plant and animal species. Agriculture has replaced native grazers with domestic livestock and substituted single-crop fields for prairie diversity. Attwater's prairie-chicken, once widespread, now booms its haunting love call from the edge of oblivion on relict islands of east Texas prairie.

Overly intensive grazing or burning will also reduce rich grassland to brushy semidesert. In parts of New Mexico, a surfeit of livestock created a waste of pavement-hard soil and thorny scrub, and the masked bobwhite, once at home there, vanished from its only United States habitat.

Amid the dominant grasses, other plants contribute to the complexity of prairie habitat. The buckeye butterfly, a ubiquitous North American grassland species, lays its eggs on plantain, vervain, figwort, and other broadleaved plants. Its young are totally dependent on those plants for food. The pronghorn of the arid western grasslands feeds on sagebrush and other broadleaved plants. Grasses may constitute as little as three percent of its diet.

Yet both the buckeye butterfly and the pronghorn depend on the burning and grazing of grasses to exist. The succulent plants they rely on are pioneers which colonize open ground. When the prairie burns, sunlight reaches their seeds, and they begin to grow. Where bison herds used to graze, they kept grasses closely cropped, further encouraging the broadleaved plants.

Grassland habitats cover from thirty to forty-five percent of the earth's land surface. Many areas, such as the American Great Plains, southern pine savannas, and high mountain meadows, are long-term grasslands as a result of geography and climate. Ephemeral grasslands are abundant, too: habitats in transition from bare ground to forest or maintained by mowing and herbicides.

Permanent grasslands don't necessarily stretch from horizon to horizon, but can develop where rock underlies shallow soil, or where high winds, frequent fires, or seasonally scarce water thwart what would otherwise be a forest ecosystem. In montane regions, grasslands, shrublands, and forests are often mixed in patterns determined by slope orientation, wind, fire, and rock outcrops.

When a forest is destroyed, an ephemeral grassland habitat may appear. Such grasslands are short-lived unless something stops the succession of plants from grasses to shrubs to forest. With the grasses, the invaders we lump together as weeds move in quickly.

Among the very best of these plant colonizers are the composites, including dandelions, daisies, and sunflowers. Many, such as black-eyed Susans and bitterweed, tolerate poor soil conditions. Falling on bare ground, seedlings quickly take control of their habitat. Their first leaves often form a large rosette flat against the ground, preventing other seeds from germinating; providing maximum exposure to the sun's rays, and minimizing moisture loss from the immediate soil microhabitat.

The dominant insects of grasslands are ants and grasshoppers. Ants feed heavily on grass seeds and various plants, some of which have adapted to limit their losses. The stems of black-eyed Susans, for example, are covered with fine hairs which impede climbing ants. While preying on grassland species, ants also benefit their habitat, aerating the soil with tunnels, fertilizing it with waste, creating bare areas for colonizing plants, and serving as food for many other animals.

Over 250 species of grasshoppers inhabit North American grasslands, and they feed primarily on grass. Left unchecked, they would devastate a grassland—and sometimes have, when drought kills off the rodents and birds that prey on them. Spiders are also abundant in grassland habitats and help control insect populations.

What is a grassland? What is a prairie? The answers are not as obvious as they seem. The scissor-tailed flycatcher, a bird of the southern Great Plains, occasionally shows up in Mississippi, where clear-cutting and agriculture have made ephemeral grasslands common. Yet the scissor-tail has not nested in these areas, but only in natural grassland, and especially in the "Black Belt Prairie" from northeastern Mississippi to south-central Alabama. Grass alone does not define the scissor-tailed flycatcher's habitat. Like all creatures, it requires a specific community of species and physical characteristics to recognize a place as habitat.

Blueberry bushes surrounded by reindeer lichen suggest a tundra habitat, but these plants grow in the Dolly Sods Wilderness Area in West Virginia. Reindeer lichen is found in tundra habitat across the northern fringe of the continent, and also extends south to isolated montane habitats where severe conditions limit invasion by other species.

Species of yellow composites, or yellow, daisylike flowers, number
25,000 worldwide, and grow mostly in grasslands, where bees and
insects pollinate them. Their abundance is not accidental. The
yellows we perceive come from carotenoid pigments which, in
sunlight, also reflect ultraviolet rays. Bees and insects see, and are
drawn to, ultraviolet light. To them, these flowers present
a pattern of yellow and a shade called ''bee purple.''

(Facing) Blooming in the Dolly Sods Wilderness,
early azaleas signal the presence of acidic soil. Most plants have
very specific tolerances for acidic or basic soils, a factor which
limits their distribution. Plants also influence the soil. Red spruce's
fallen needles in the Dolly Sods add acid as they decompose,
improving conditions for azaleas.

(Facing) The mule deer, North America's largest deer, ranges from Canada to Mexico. The cougar is its main predator. In this century, numbers of cougars have drastically declined; mule deer have accordingly prospered. Family groups range over a few square miles, feeding on broad-leaved plants and grasses at dawn and dusk and resting in sheltered areas at night and during the heat of the day.

The grasslands of the Great Basin are home to the pronghorn, a unique native American species with no close living relatives. Once pronghorns numbered in the millions, but by the 1920s, only a few thousand remained. Uncontrolled hunting was one cause; the bison's disappearance was another. Bison feed largely on grass, pronghorns on low, broad-leaved herbaceous plants. Without grazing bison, grass grew tall, shading out the pronghorn's food supply.

In tundra regions like this area near Hudson Bay in Manitoba, no trees can take root. Repeated thaws and freezes churn rocks and soil near the surface, and permanently frozen earth begins a few inches down. Despite high winds, bitter cold, and long, dark winters, some life thrives. Lichens that may live for centuries slowly break rock into soil. Tiny willows, only inches high, provide cover and food for lemmings and snowshoe hares.

A thousand miles south of the nearest tundra and permafrost, heathlands in West Virginia's Dolly Sods Wilderness Area have a tundralike appearance. Fierce winds are the cause. Reindeer lichens thrive at some sites, and the huckleberries, blueberries, goldenrod, and other vegetation that take hold remain low and stunted.

A black-and-yellow argiope spider hangs upside down waiting for an insect to strike her sticky web. This spider's vision is poor; web vibrations tell her when and where an insect lands. Then she races to the spot and wraps up the victim for a later meal. A courting male spider who visits treads lightly, informing the female of his presence by lightly plucking strands of the web. If disturbed, she may drop to the ground to hide.

(Facing) On a spring day in the Everglades' Taylor Slough, an orb-weaving spider maintains her web. In the deep south, orb weavers' lacy nets appear throughout the year, as the mature adults who weave them do not die in winter frosts.

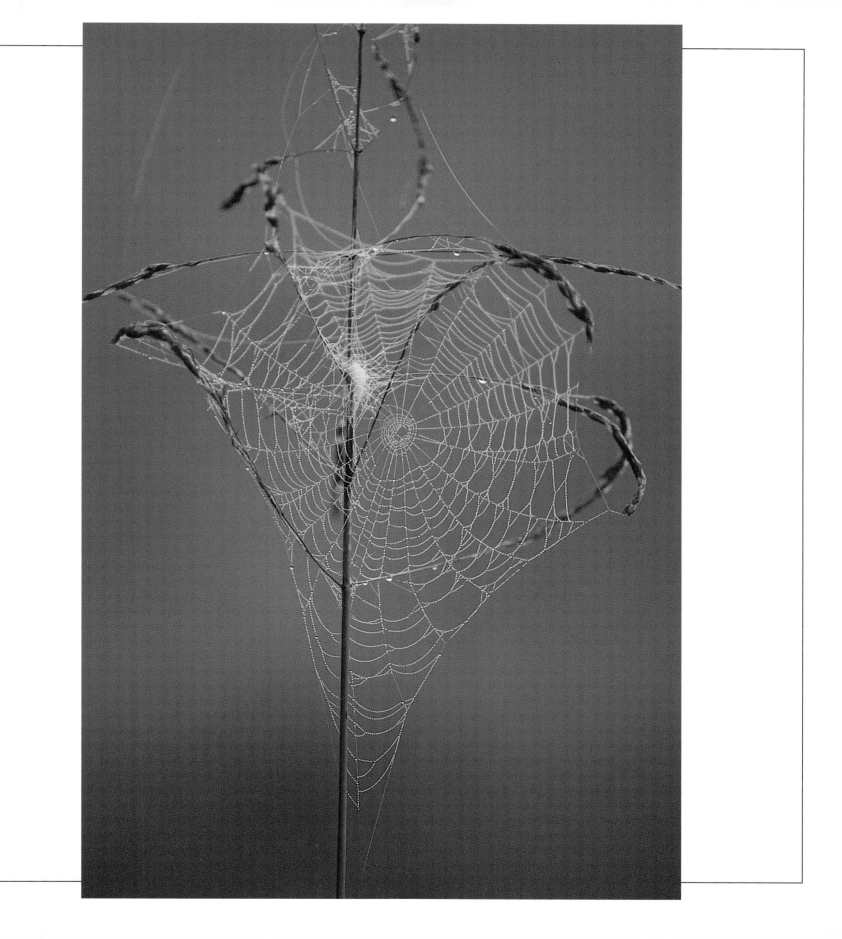

A Savannah sparrow, heading for its nest with food in its beak, looks for predators from the curly dock's seed head in a North Dakota grassland. A weed to fastidious keepers of lawns, curly dock is an excellent winter source of seeds to the Savannah sparrow and many other birds.

(Facing) For centuries, Plains Indians coexisted with American bison, depending on them for meat and hides and gathering their dung for fuel. Between 1865 and 1900, buffalo hunters and settlers almost brought the huge herbivore to extinction, shooting them for sport, slaughtering them to deprive the Indians of their livelihood, and turning their short-grass prairie habitat into farmland.

(Facing) Theodore Roosevelt established the National Bison Range NWR on the west slope of the Montana Rockies at a time when fewer than 300 American bison remained in the wild. Today the refuge provides habitat for a thriving bison herd and other large mammals, including Rocky Mountain bighorn sheep.

Often seen in National Bison Range NWR, the agile Rocky Mountain bighorn sheep eludes pursuers by crossing rock slides and leaping from one tiny rock ledge to another. To further minimize predation, the bighorn rapidly consumes a great amount of food in a grassy meadow, then retires to chew its cud in rocky areas with a good view of surrounding terrain.

I thought the sparrow's note from heaven,
Singing at dawn on the alder bough;
I brought him home, in his nest, at even;
He sings the song, but it cheers not now,
For I did not bring home the river and sky;—
He sang to my ear,—they sang to my eye.

As I spoke, beneath my feet
The ground-pine curled its pretty wreath,
Running over the club-moss burrs;
I inhaled the violet's breath;
Around me stood the oaks and firs;
Pine-cones and acorns lay on the ground;
Over me soared the eternal sky,
Full of light and of deity;
Again I saw, again I heard,
The rolling river, the morning bird;—
Beauty through my senses stole;
I yielded myself to the perfect whole.

Ralph Waldo Emerson
From "Each and All," 1839

Index